$2.25

Kungfu
FOR
KIDS

paulEng

Tuttle Publishing
Boston • Rutland, Vermont • Tokyo

Special thanks to
Andrew and Ryan Tom
for posing for the drawings,
to Gary Tom, David Taran, and
Don Hopkins, and to Martha Dahlen
for help in writing the text.

IMPORTANT NOTE TO READERS:
Training in the martial arts involves physical exertion,
movements and actions that can cause injury to you or others.
Because the physical activities in this book may be too strenuous
for some readers, you should check with a physician before you
start your training. If you are ever in doubt about how to
proceed or about whether a practice is safe for you, consult a
martial arts professional before proceeding.

First published in 2005 by Tuttle Publishing, an imprint of
Periplus Editions (HK) Ltd., with editorial offices at
153 Milk Street, Boston, Massachusetts 02109.

Library of Congress Cataloging-in-Publication Data

Eng, Paul.
   Kungfu for kids / Paul Eng.—1st. ed.
        p. cm.
   ISBN 0-8048-3600-0 (hardcover)
   1. Kung fu—Juvenile literature. I. Title.
GV1114.7.E534 2004
796.815'9—dc22   2004007244

DISTRIBUTED BY

North America, Latin America, and Europe
Tuttle Publishing
Distribution Center
Airport Business Park
364 Innovation Drive
North Clarendon, VT 05759-9436
Tel: (802) 773-8930
Fax: (802) 773-6993
email: info@tuttlepublishing.com
www.tuttlepublishing.com

Japan
Tuttle Publishing
Yaekari Building, 3rd Floor
5-4-12 Ōsaki
Shinagawa-ku
Tokyo 141 0032
Tel: (03) 5437-0171
Fax: (03) 5437-0755
email: tuttle-sales@gol.com

Asia Pacific
Berkeley Books Pte. Ltd.
130 Joo Seng Road
#06-01/03 Olivine Building
Singapore 368357
Tel: (65) 6280-1330
Fax: (65) 6280-6290
email: inquiries@periplus.com.sg
www.periplus.com

First edition
10 09 08 07 06 05   10 9 8 7 6 5 4 3 2 1
Printed in Malaysia

Illustrations by Stephanie Tok
Design by Kathryn Sky-Peck

CONTENTS

one

WHAT IS KUNGFU?

Do you want to learn kungfu? Do you know what kungfu really is? Kungfu is a Chinese martial art. The word *martial* means it has to do with fighting or combat. The word *art* means that it is part technique (what can be learned) and part personal expression (what is unique to the person doing it). So, kungfu is both an effective fighting method and a beautiful way of moving.

Finally, kungfu is Chinese, which means it is part of Chinese culture. In fact, kungfu is one of the oldest parts of Chinese culture. It began as military exercises for soldiers, then it became exercises for Buddhist monks. Eventually, it developed into many fighting styles. Have you heard of *Shaolin*? The history of kungfu explains why Shaolin styles are so famous and why many styles are named after animals.

HISTORY OF KUNGFU

The history of kungfu had four main periods. Let's take a look at each.

The Age of Military Arts (1600 B.C.–A.D. 500)
In the earliest days, exercises were developed mainly to prepare soldiers for battle. Some of these exercises were performed like dances to music.

The Age of Shaolin (500–1644)
In A.D. 495, a Buddhist temple was built on a mountain in eastern China and named Shaolin (the name means "Little Forest"). Soon, a monk named Bodhidharma came from India to teach a new practice (what was to become Zen Buddhism). But Bodhidharma found that his students were too weak to meditate long hours, and they fell asleep! He feared that they would never achieve anything this way, so he created exercises to strengthen them. The exercises worked!

After Bodhidharma died, the Shaolin temple monks continued to practice the exercises. Sometimes, bandits attacked their temple. When the monks defeated these bandits, they became famous for their fighting skills. Soon people outside the temple began to learn the exercises too. To improve the techniques, masters watched wild animals and insects fighting. Then they used the animals' strategies and techniques to improve and expand Bodhidharma's system.

The Age of Dispersion (1644–1910)
In 1644, Manchurians invaded China and overthrew the Ming Dynasty. The Manchurians feared that the Shaolin monks would help Ming supporters start a rebellion, so they burned the Shaolin temple and tried to stamp out its kungfu. Only

a few monks survived. Most of them fled to southern China, especially Canton province, and to parts of Southeast Asia, such as Vietnam and Thailand. There they established schools, but each school was a little different. From these schools, students left to set up even more schools. There was no way to keep the styles and techniques the same, so gradually many styles of kungfu developed. The styles are like the branches of a tree: they have a common root (the Shaolin system) but are otherwise independent and often very different.

The Modern Age of Kungfu and Wushu

After the invention of guns, kungfu was mainly practiced as a sport. At the turn of the twentieth century (1900), there was much debate: should China adopt Western exercises and competitive sports or keep its martial arts? Eventually the Chinese decided to keep both, with two branches of the martial arts—one for competition and one for tradition. The traditional form is called *kungfu*, a Cantonese term. It emphasizes self-defense and fighting applications; it is what you see in movies. The other branch, the modern form, is called *wushu*. Wushu is mainly for competition and demonstrations, so it has more acrobatic movements; it is what you see in the Olympics and public performances. The International Committee of Wushu, with its headquarters in Beijing, the capital of China, creates the forms for wushu practice.

Praying Mantis Kungfu

One of the most famous Shaolin styles is called Praying Mantis Kungfu. This was created by a monk named Wang Long. Walking through a forest one day, Wang Long happened to see a praying mantis fight a much larger insect, the cicada. Due to its speed and special forearm movements, the praying mantis won. Wang Long studied the praying mantis's movements and then created a system based on what he learned. Praying Mantis is now one of the most famous and effective styles of kungfu.

Wushu vs. Kungfu

Wu shu is actually the correct term or translation of the term "martial arts." *Kungfu* is a general term that means "concentrated effort"; it can apply to anything that requires hard work. Kungfu came to mean martial arts when people in Canton province saw how hard fighters practiced. As a joke, they called them "kungfu" fighters. When Hong Kong film studios began using martial arts in movies, the movies were called "kungfu movies," and the name is now known all over the world.

STYLES OF KUNGFU

Kungfu has many styles: some are vigorous; others appear more quiet. Some emphasize footwork; others emphasize hand, arm, and elbow work. The most common styles of kungfu taught outside of China are described below.

Northern Styles

Long Fist ("Chang Quan"): This is considered the original kungfu system. It is good for general health, for competitions, and as a foundation for learning weapons forms later.

Northern Praying Mantis ("Tong Long"): This is also an old style, with many forms suitable for all body types.

Monkey: This style is based on the typical movements of monkeys. Its forms involve a lot of tumbling and rolling.

Southern Styles

Hung Family ("Hung Gar"): This is one of the most famous and popular southern styles; it is good for all ages and body types.

Choy Li Fut: This is a relatively new style, with many different hand and weapon forms.

Wing Chun: This is a relatively simple style, but very effective, and particularly good for those wanting to learn self-defense. It is very popular, with many schools. (It is the style the famous actor Bruce Lee learned.)

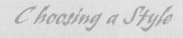

Choosing a Style

What if you really want to learn a style, but there is no school teaching that style in your area? Don't let this stop you. In the beginning, you will learn almost the same skills no matter what style you study. So just pick the best school with the best instructor available, learn the basics well, and then you will be able to pick up any style later.

two
GETTING READY

To get ready for kungfu classes, you need to prepare two things: the right clothes and the right attitude.

WHAT TO WEAR

The clothes you need will depend on your school. Some schools ask their students to wear uniforms; other schools allow students to wear what they like. If there is a uniform, then the school usually sells it. If there is no uniform, then these guidelines will help you choose the right clothes.

Shoes

The best shoes are sturdy but light and flexible. Make sure your ankles can move freely. The soles should be thick enough for you to stomp comfortably, but thin enough for you to slide when needed. No metal buckles! (Hint: Many people find that skateboard shoes are ideal.)

Pants

Traditional kungfu pants are made of cotton with elastic at the ankles and a drawstring at the waist. They must be loose so that you can easily spread your legs wide for kicks and jumps, but not so loose that they might fall off or get in your way.

Sashes

In some traditional schools, only advanced students and teachers wear sashes, and the sashes are always black. In some modern schools, all students wear sashes, and colors are used to indicate rank, like the belt system in karate.

The Multipurpose Sash

The sash is more than a fancy belt for holding your pants up. Originally, it had three other purposes. First, when tied tightly, it supported the lower back and breathing center. Second, it was used to hide small weapons. Third, where the sash was tied (right, left, or center) indicated the wearer's rank.

Make Your School Proud!

What you wear should make your school proud to have you as its student. This means:

- **Clean.** Always wear clean clothes/uniform—without holes or tears.

- **Neat.** Your clothes/uniform should fit properly.

- **Loyal.** Never wear a uniform from another school or another martial art.

Shirts

In most schools cotton T-shirts are worn in the summer and sweatshirts in the winter. If your school doesn't have a shirt with its logo, then wear what other students wear. Most likely, a plain black shirt is best.

Special Events

For tournaments and demonstrations, colored or special shirts or uniforms may be required. In these cases, the school will tell you beforehand what you need and where to buy it.

Equipment

Beginners generally do not need any extra equipment. Later, when you start sparring (working with a partner), you will need protective equipment. When that time comes, your teacher should let you know what you need.

ATTITUDE

When you come to the kungfu school, you should not only wear the right clothes, but you should also wear the right attitude. Both the right clothes and the right attitude will help you make quick progress.

The right attitude has these parts:

Respect. Respect begins with appreciation. Think of your teacher's patience and effort in teaching you. Think of your fellow students and how much you are just like them. Think of the art itself, passed down since the days of the Shaolin Temple! Then show your appreciation as respect.

Patience. You need patience with other people *and* with yourself. Is the teacher going too fast? Too slow? Do you find one week you can do something very well, and the next week you can't do it at all? Patience begins with understanding. Know this:

- The physical process of growth can upset your balance and coordination. So what you can do one month may not be so easy next month, until your body gets used to its new size.

- The first time is always the hardest. Often you will find that the second time you try to do or remember something, it is easier. This is natural. Don't give up or get discouraged after only one or two tries!

- Learning occurs in spurts. That is, in the beginning you may make quick progress. Then, for a long time, you may see (or feel) no change. Then, suddenly, again you advance quickly. Be prepared, mentally, for these cycles. Work steadily, and have confidence that the next spurt of progress is just around the corner.

- Other people are just like you. Just as you want people to adjust to your speed, so they want you to adjust to their speed. Have patience.

Determination. Keep at it! The more difficult the challenge, the more valuable the reward. Keep practicing and you will be proud of your achievement!

three
THE KUNGFU SCHOOL

A kungfu school is a cross between a school and a home. Just as there are rules in your school and your home, there are also rules and customs to follow in the kungfu school. Your school will not be exactly like what we describe, but these notes should help you know what to expect.

DESCRIPTION

Most kungfu schools consist of a big open area for training, together with a teacher's office and changing rooms. Along the walls you may see equipment for working out— punching bags, weights, bars. You will also probably see many weapons and trophies.

Somewhere in the room you are likely to see a picture or a statue of a big Chinese man with a red face, a huge sword, and a blue horse. This is Gwan Gung, or General Gwan. He was a great general during the Three Kingdoms period of ancient China and a renowned kungfu fighter. He is respected as the patron saint of both the martial arts and justice. Sometimes he has two other people with him: one is his adopted son; the other, his sword bearer.

On the walls you are also likely to find Chinese writing. Ask your teacher what the words mean: they are usually traditional phrases that are meant to inspire you as you train.

RULES AND ETIQUETTE

A kungfu school needs some rules to help everyone live and work happily together. As soon as you join a school, ask if they have a list of rules and read them carefully. Then try to follow them. Even if you fail, everyone will appreciate your effort.

How to Act in Class

Arrive on time.

Ask questions only at the appropriate time. Do not chatter during class. This means both during instruction and during training. After class is the time to make friends with your fellow students.

Do not eat or chew gum.

Wear only your uniform—don't wear a hat or sunglasses or rings or a watch or any other kind of jewelry. These things can get

Traditional Training Develops Kungfu Spirit

The kungfu movie star Jackie Chan learned kungfu in a traditional opera training school in Hong Kong. In the school, students trained all day long, from early in the morning until evening. Not only that, as one of the older students, Jackie was held responsible for how well the younger students performed. If they did poorly, he was punished! With respect for his teachers, patience with his fellow students, and determination, he was able to become the star he is today.

in the way, and possibly hurt you and anyone you work with.

Do not handle any of the equipment in the school until you are invited to or instructed to. Many schools have various kinds of weight training and muscle developing devices; leave them alone! You will be shown how to use them at the proper time.

Do not handle any weapons that do not belong to you. Most schools have racks of all kinds of weapons—staffs, swords, sabers, and chains—on display. They are all really cool, but (1) they are dangerous and (2) they do not belong to you! Leave them alone until you are instructed in how to use them. (The time will come. Be patient!)

How to Act Toward Teachers

Show respect to your teachers at all times. Whenever they give instruction, thank them—you may bow and/or give the salute in appreciation.

Do not ask the teacher to teach you something in particular, or to teach you more often or faster. Even though you may be eager to learn something new and you're sure you have mastered what you have been taught, or you are just tired of what you are practicing, you should wait. Your teacher has had many years of experience teaching; he knows what is best. So keep practicing and let him decide what you should learn and when.

How to Act Toward Fellow Students

Show respect to all of your fellow students, no matter how good or bad you think they are.

Do not correct or criticize other people—not to their face or behind their back. If you see someone else doing something that you think is wrong, do not correct him or her. Instead, ask an instructor to make sure that *you* are not doing something wrong.

Do not compare yourself or your progress with other students. Do not think poorly of those who seem to be worse than you. Similarly, do not show off. Neither of these attitudes will help you improve. No matter how well you are doing, there is someone who is better; no matter how poorly you think you are doing, there is someone even worse. To compare wastes time; just work hard.

As a new student, older students will help you. As an older student, you will be expected to help younger students.

How to Act in Public

Remember, you are a representative of your school: how you behave reflects on your teacher and your fellow students. If you bring shame on yourself, you bring shame on your school.

Do not brag, show off, or pick fights. Do not let people make you angry. An attack with words may be as painful as an attack with a fist, but a true martial artist avoids fighting. Learn to act in a way that will solve problems—and make your teacher proud of you. Remember, you are a representative of your school at all times.

four
THE CLASS

Salute, side view

Naturally, schools of kungfu differ. Some are big and modern; some are small and traditional. Some teach everyone in large groups; others divide into smaller groups for workouts. Either way, there are certain activities that you can expect to find in any school's classes. The following sections describe what you can expect in a typical class.

THE SALUTE

Usually a class will begin with a salute to the teacher. The class may also salute photographs of former masters. This is important. You salute them because you want to show appreciation for their hard work that has made it possible for you to also learn and because you respect them. You must learn the particular salute of your school.

The Secret Ming Salute

One common salute is to place the right fist in the palm of the left hand, holding the two hands in front of the chest. This salute comes from the days of the Manchurian dynasty when the Ming people were rebels (see Chapter 1). To identify each other, Ming rebels used this salute because it represented the word *ming* in the Chinese language. This

Salute, front view

word is comprised of the word for "sun" (represented by the fist) and the word for "moon" (represented by the open palm).

WARM-UPS

After the salute come warm-up exercises. These are important for two reasons. First, you need to get your body ready for exercise. Warming up helps make sure you will do your best and not get hurt. Second, you need to "change channels" in your mind: change from home-school-friends and tune in to the kungfu channel.

At school, your teacher will probably lead the class in doing warm-up and stretching exercises. If you arrive early, or if you are practicing at home, you can devise your own warm-ups. Basically, the goal is to warm every muscle, loosen every joint, and get your heart beating a little faster. Here is a sample routine; it starts at your head and works down to your toes.

First, turn your head gently from side to side, loosening the neck. Then move your shoulders, up, down, and around, in big cir-

cles, in both directions. Shake your arms and hands, even loosening your fingers! Swing your arms in big circles, like the propellers on an airplane. Then move your hips and waist in circles, first out to the left, then out to the right. Put your hands on your knees and move them in circles, first clockwise and then counterclockwise. Finally, stand on one leg with the toe tips of the other leg on the ground and circle your ankle; repeat on the other side.

Now it is time to get blood moving. You may jump up and down (like skipping rope), perhaps twisting from side to side. Or you may do jumping jacks. Or you may simply run in place.

Finally, do some stretching exercises. Side bends and forward bends (touching your toes) are good examples.

At the end of warm-ups, your body should be warm and loose, and your mind totally focused on the great kungfu you are about to learn.

DRILLS

One important part of any training session is drills. Usually, the drills are designed by the chief instructor. They will be based on the basic movements—front stance, forward punch, thrust kick, and so on—and will be made up of the basic movements, repeated in different ways. You may find these a little boring, but they really build strong muscles fast. And because they are basic movements, they will build exactly

Poke Stance

A typical kungfu leg stretch is to squat on one leg and stretch the other leg out to the side. This is called the poke stance. Try to keep both feet flat on the floor and your back straight. Then shift to the other side.

the muscles you need for the kungfu you will do later.

FORMS

The forms are the second essential and traditional part of kungfu training. Each form represents a fight and is made up of a sequence of movements that you must memorize. Unlike a fight, with a form your opponent is invisible! You have to imagine what he is doing as you perform the movements. There are many forms: some are long, some short; some are difficult, some easy. Beginners' forms are short and simple; more advanced forms are long and complicated.

HOW TO PARTICIPATE

While each school is different, the methods of learning are the same. First, you must listen. Do not chatter to your neighbor. Do not look around the room. Do not think about your homework due tomorrow. Just listen to your instructor.

Second, you must observe. This is probably the most critical skill of all—and it is something that your body does, *not* your mind. So, turn off your mind—don't let it interfere with thoughts of first this, then that. Instead, just watch. Let your whole body be your eyes. Let your mind become a picture of what you are seeing.

Third, you must copy. Bring back to your mind the picture of your teacher's demonstration—as though it were on a bulletin board

Crouching Tiger, Hidden Dragon

This phrase is the title of a famous movie, but it has another meaning. A hidden dragon is someone who has great skill but doesn't show it. A crouching tiger is someone who is quiet but very alert; when the time is right, he springs into action. In this way, for both dragon and tiger, surprise makes strength even more powerful.

in front of your nose. Then, do the action. In this way, your body will naturally perform the movements as you have seen them.

Fourth, you must repeat—over and over and over and over—until the movements become automatic.

This is the only way to become really good. There are no substitutes or shortcuts. When you repeat, you gradually develop power, coordination, balance, and gracefulness—all the things that make kungfu great. To stick with the training, you need patience and perseverance and determination—and these are part of the internal training. So have confidence that you are progressing in every way as you practice again and again.

13

SPARRING

Sparring is practice fighting with another person. This usually comes later in your training. After learning one-man forms you will learn two-man forms. They you will have a chance to spar using the techniques you have learned. There are rules to make sure that you and your partner don't hurt each other and to keep the fight fair. You will see this at your school and then have a chance to do it later in your training.

COOL DOWN

After your workout, you should take time to cool down. Just like the warm-up period, the cool down period has two purposes. The first purpose is to rest your body; the second purpose is to help your mind switch gears. This time you need to switch from kungfu "gear" back to the real-world "gear" of friends, home, and school.

Your teacher probably has his own approach to cooling down. One way is to lie down, with arms and legs spread, and relax your whole body. Feel your arms and legs sink into the floor like heavy weights. Another way is to walk slowly around the training room. In this case, feel how light your body is. Imagine a hook at the top of your head attached to a balloon on a string. The balloon lifts your body so that you float as you walk. Yet another way is to sit cross-legged, very still and very straight. In this case you may imagine the balloon lifting your head and spine, while your legs and lower body sink into the floor.

In all cases, breathe deeply and don't think of anything—just feel your whole body warm and happy!

Cool Down Key

The key to cooling down is to relax totally. Some people achieve this by feeling very light; other people relax by feeling very heavy. Either way, there should not be even one muscle working.

FINAL SALUTE

Finally, give the salute again, to your teachers and past masters, showing your respect and gratitude for this chance to study kungfu.

SAFETY

To make sure your training is safe, here are three things to remember when you get hurt or hurt yourself:

1. Not all pain means gain. Have you heard the expression "No pain, no gain"? When people say this, they mean that if you don't hurt a little when you exercise, you are probably not getting any benefit. This is only true sometimes. You need to learn to know when pain is an alarm bell and when it is not.

An example of "good" pain, or pain you don't need to worry about, is aching muscles after you have done more push-ups than you have ever done before. You have to stretch your muscles to make them grow, so they will feel a little sore when you make them do more than they are used to. A little sore is okay; you can keep exercising, if you are careful.

An example of bad pain is when you twist your ankle or pull a muscle. This kind of pain is often sharp and sudden. In this case, the pain is a warning that something is seriously wrong. It is like a fire alarm in your house: if you ignore it when there's a real fire, then the whole house could burn down. Likewise, if you ignore pain that is a warning of a serious injury, you could cause great damage if you keep exercising.

If you have an injury or any pain that you're not sure of, tell your parent or your instructor. Let them help you decide whether it's best to keep exercising or to rest.

2. Prevention is better than cure. When anything breaks, fixing it takes a lot of time. And usually it's no fun waiting for the thing to be fixed. Your body is the same way. Breaking a bone or spraining an ankle can occur in a split second—and then take weeks or months to heal!

3. Accidents happen. The final piece of advice to remember is that, no matter how hard people try to be safe, accidents will happen. There are three important rules to follow when an accident occurs. First, don't blame anyone. No one is trying to hurt anyone. Accidents simply happen. Second, take care of the physical problem right away. Tell your teacher, and let him or her handle it. Third, learn from the accident. How did it happen? Try to see how it could have been avoided, and then make sure you don't create that situation again.

If you have an injury, tell your teacher or your mother or father—let him or her decide what to do next. Usually, injuries can be healed most quickly and easily just after they have happened.

Sprain vs. Strain

Strains and sprains are the most common kinds of injuries in kungfu. **A strain is a pulled muscle.** Ouch! The area around the strain will become very sore and swell up. The best remedy is to stop using it. At the beginning you may apply ice, wrapped in a cloth, off and on, until the swelling goes down. Then rest. Mild strains usually heal in a week.

Sprains, like a twisted ankle, are more serious. They involve the ligaments that connect bones to bones at a joint. Usually they happen after a fall or misstep. As with sprains, the best remedy is to stop using the joint and put ice on it, off and on, until the swelling goes down. Sprains take much longer to heal. Give a sprain at least three to four weeks before you use that joint in a normal way.

To Prevent Injury

1. **Always warm up.**

2. When learning something new, **watch and follow directions carefully.** Don't rush to do it, thinking it looks easy. This is especially true when learning new kicks.

3. If you are afraid of trying something new—especially **if you think you might get hurt—then don't do it!** Wait. Watch other people do it until you have more confidence. Tell your instructor and he will help.

4. **Always keep your mind on what you are doing**—and be aware of what your neighbor is doing so you don't hurt each other by mistake.

5. **If you feel pain, stop!** Ask your teacher if you are doing the movement the right way. Continue only when you are sure you are doing it correctly.

five
BASIC ELEMENTS

Kungfu trains the whole person, inside and out. So, what does *that* mean? The outside is the physical body. This is what you can see and touch; it is the flesh and bones that move and act. The inside is the mind and spirit. This is what you can't see or touch; it feels and thinks. Learning kungfu can make your body strong and fit. It can also help keep your mind calm and alert and it can help you develop virtue.

The first part of this chapter describes the outside, or "external," physical training. This consists of the basic movements (blocks, punches, kicks, and so on) and the forms (sequences of movements, sort of like dances). The second half of the chapter describes the inside or "internal" training of kungfu. No action here—how boring, right? No! Your spirit is the commander in chief; your mind is the general: only with proper training can the commander and general be sure to lead the army to victory. Enjoy all of your training!

Horse stance

HORSE STANCE

This stance is a basic stance not only for kungfu but also for most Asian martial arts. It strengthens your knees, opens your hip joints so you can move your legs more freely, gives you a sense of stability—and develops courage, the Chinese say.

To find the position, stand with your feet together. Then move both toe tips out (pivot or turn on your heels); then move both heels out (pivot on your toes); and then move both toe tips out again (pivot on your heels). Stop!

Your feet should be parallel, a little wider than your shoulders. Bend your knees to lower your body: this is called sinking into position. Let your upper body relax but keep your back straight. Keep your hands as fists at your waist, with your elbows back. On each breath, let your chest expand and totally fill with air—all the way down to your belly. You should feel very solid, like a big tree rooted to the ground. See how long you can stay in position. (At the Shaolin Temple, young kungfu students were asked to "sit" in the horse stance for an hour or more!)

FORWARD STANCE

The forward stance is the second most common stance in Asian martial arts. It is used to deliver power through the front.

To find the position, start from a horse stance. Then pivot on the balls of the feet either to the left or right. For a right forward stance, turn your body to the right, and turn your feet so that they both point at an angle (about 45 degrees) to the left. The toe tip of the front foot should be in a line with the heel of the back foot. As with the horse stance, you can keep your hands as fists at your waist. Expand your chest, but keep your upper body (especially your shoulders) relaxed. Feel strong!

CAT OR TIGER STANCE

From this stance, you should be ready to pounce in any direction.

To find the position, you may start from a forward stance. Then, sit back until all of your weight is over your back leg. Bring your front leg back, bend the knee, and set just the tips of your toes on the ground in front of you. To make the stance more stable, your toe tips should be to the side and not directly in front of the other foot. Both knees should be slightly bent so that you look and feel alert—ready to counter your opponent's next move.

Forward stance

Tiger stance

17

CROSS OR X-STANCE

In this stance, you may feel that your legs are twisted like pretzels, but it is a valuable stance for moving forward, backward, or sideways.

Cross stance

To find the position, set one foot facing forward. Then slide the other leg behind it, and set the toes and ball of your foot down, heel up. Most (but not quite all) of your weight should be on the front leg, with one knee behind the other. Look backward, over the raised heel, and try to keep your upper body erect, relaxed, and alert.

CRANE STANCE

Like a big bird, you must have good balance for this one. The crane stance is used to prepare for kicks and hops.

To find the position, you may start from a cat stance. With all of your weight on your back leg, raise the front, bent leg until its toes just touch the opposite knee. Keep your toes pointed toward the ground. Your back leg should be straight, but the knee should not be locked. Keep your back straight, shoulders down; keep alert, and keep your balance.

Crane stance

HAND TECHNIQUES

In kungfu, "hand" can mean the whole arm. Fingers, hands, fists, elbows, shoulders, and arms can be used to block, trap, punch, deflect, grab, claw, push, and jab. Thus, these are the fastest and most versatile natural weapons you have. Many styles of kungfu have very particular hand and fist forms—such as the tiger claw in the Fu Jow Pai style and the mantis hand in the Praying Mantis style. Below we will describe only a few of the most basic and common forms.

WILLOW LEAF PALM

This is an example of an open-hand technique. The four fingers are kept straight, tightly pressed together, with the thumb bent and held firmly against the palm. The wrist is slightly bent. All sides of the palm can be used. That is, you may strike with the inside or outside edges, the heel of the hand, or the back of the hand. You may thrust with the fingers, keeping the wrist straight.

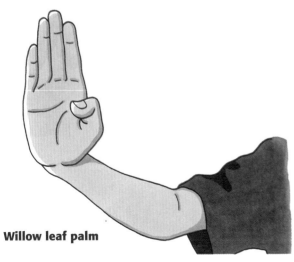

Willow leaf palm

In all cases, be sure to keep your fingers together and the thumb bent out of the way.

CLOSED HAND FLAT FIST

This is probably the most basic hand form for any style of fighting. Close your four fingers into your palm, then fold your thumb over your fingers. There are three important points.

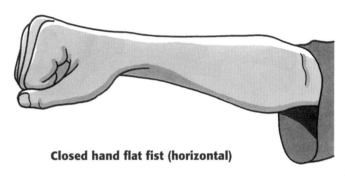

Closed hand flat fist (horizontal)

First, do not simply clench your fist as tightly as you can. Instead, hold your fingers so that the knuckles of your four fingers make a flat surface (you may press your fist against the wall or a table to check its flatness). Second, do not let the tip of your thumb stick out beyond your knuckles. The thumb should be bent and held back behind the front of the knuckles. Third, your wrist must be straight. When the wrist is straight it is strong, it cannot be broken, and it can deliver full power from the shoulder and elbow.

The fist can be used in two positions. That is, it can be held with the thumb on top. This is called a vertical fist and is used for a vertical punch. Or it can be held with the thumb at the side. This is called a horizontal fist and is used for a horizontal punch.

EAGLE CLAW

The eagle claw is common to both northern and southern styles of kungfu. It is used to grip and grab. To make the claw, hold your four fingers together and bend them at the two upper knuckles (but not at the base of the knuckles, where the fingers join the hand). Hold your thumb off to the side, and bend it in the same way. Then bend your whole hand back at the wrist.

Eagle claw

STRAIGHT PUNCH

This is exactly what the name says: a punch straight forward. The fist can be vertical (thumb on top) or horizontal (thumb to the side). When you punch, don't let your fist go out to the full extent of your arm; just go about 90 percent. As soon as it reaches that point, let your fist bounce back a little, and then immediately pull your arm back. Let your arm be a little elastic, like a rubber band. Never lock your elbow! Also, when you punch, have your target in mind.

Is it high? Low? Are you aiming at an opponent's chin? Chest? Keep your mind and body alert, both focused on what you are doing.

BACK FIST

In this technique, the back of the fist strikes the target and the elbow is held still. (Hint: Doing a back fist is like drawing a circle in the air with your fist while your elbow stays still.) For the simplest version, you may start from a forward stance with your arms held

Back fist

in an "on guard" position in front of your body. Make a fist with your striking hand. Then, holding your elbow as still as you can, circle or "twirl" your forearm down, up and out, and strike the target with the back of your fist. Remember to keep a good fist—with the thumb tucked and the wrist straight.

UPPERCUT

This movement is used to strike a target from below. Hold the striking arm at the side of your body, with the hand in a fist, knuckles down, thumb and palm up. Then swing the arm up, delivering a rising blow. The uppercut is usually aimed either to the chin or the stomach of an opponent. Keep your target in mind, and don't let your arm swing up very much beyond that.

CIRCULAR BLOCK

The purpose of a block is to move an incoming blow to the side so that it misses you. This is called deflecting the blow. Your hand can be in any position—either as a fist, palm, or claw. Imagine an opponent's punch coming straight toward you. To block

Uppercut

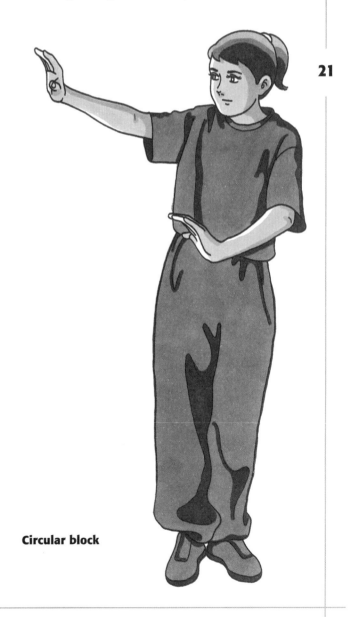

Circular block

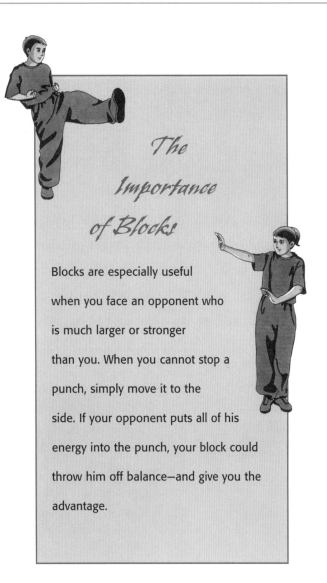

The Importance of Blocks

Blocks are especially useful when you face an opponent who is much larger or stronger than you. When you cannot stop a punch, simply move it to the side. If your opponent puts all of his energy into the punch, your block could throw him off balance—and give you the advantage.

swing your elbow straight up. After you try this a few times, you will feel its power. You will also see that the flexibility of the shoulder is very important. If your shoulder is loose, then the elbow can move farther and deliver more power. Again, as with other punches and strikes, do not let your elbow travel as far as it can. Stop at about 90 percent, let it bounce back a little, and then immediately pull it back.

it, your arm will move in a circle in front of your body. For an outside circular block, your forearm will move from a lower to a higher position. For an inside block, your forearm will move from high to low.

ELBOW STRIKE

The elbow can deliver powerful blows. When the arm is bent it is very solid, it is not easily broken, and it can deliver full force from the shoulder. For a straight elbow strike, hold your arm at your side, then bring your hand up to your shoulder. To strike,

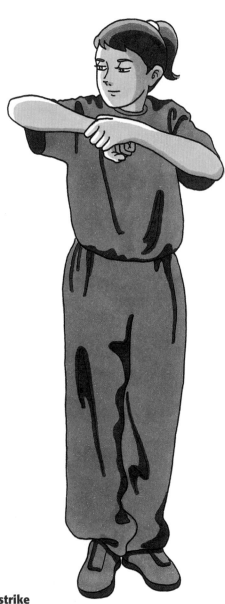

Elbow strike

K I C K S

FRONT SNAP OR GROIN KICK

This is the most basic kick, but it is not easy to do well. Use this kick to learn to coordinate your upper and lower body. Try to keep good balance before, during, and after the kick.

To perform a front kick, shift your weight to the nonkicking leg, lift the knee of the kicking leg, bring the lower leg forward, and finally snap your foot out. There are three important points to keep in mind. First, the kick should snap out from the knee; do not swing your whole leg from the hip. Second, use the top of your foot to hit the target; do not strike with your toes. Third, bring your lower leg back right after the kick. If you leave your leg stretched out, your opponent can easily grab your leg and throw you over.

LOW KICK

This is a fast, easy, and effective kick. It is particularly useful because it is less dangerous for the person doing the kicking.

Do a front low kick just like you do a front snap kick. The difference is that, here, you should aim low, at your opponent's knee, shin, or ankle. For a front low kick,

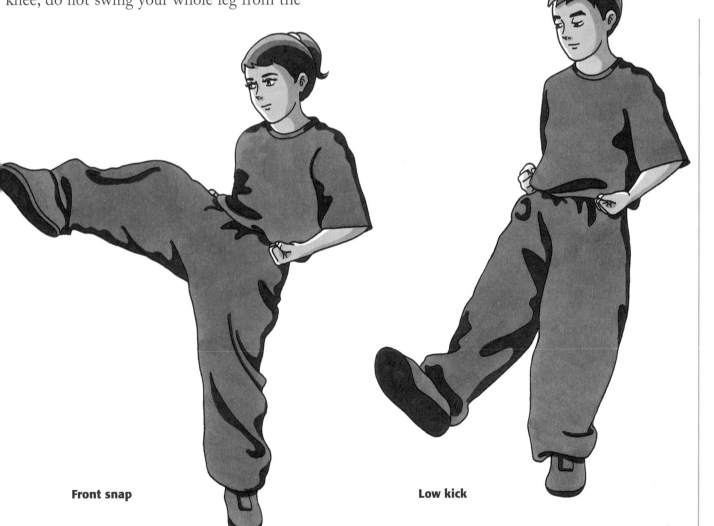

Front snap

Low kick

first shift your weight to the nonkicking leg, then snap the kick out from the knee. For a back low kick, lift the kicking leg—but not too high—and then thrust it backward, keeping your foot bent at the ankle so that the heel leads the kick. In that way, the power is sent out through the strong heel.

HEEL OR THRUST KICK

Compared to the front snap kick, the thrust kick is slower but more powerful. Try to focus the strength of both legs and the body through the heel of the kicking foot.

To perform a heel kick, shift your weight to the nonkicking leg and bend that knee as though getting ready to jump. Lift the knee of the kicking leg and bend the toes back toward your body. Then, at the same time, thrust your raised heel toward the target and straighten the nonkicking leg. Keep your balance! The two legs must work together, and you must keep your balance in order to deliver a strong kick. As soon as the kick is finished, pull your foot back so that your opponent cannot grab it.

SIDE KICK

This is a very strong kick, but probably better used for tournaments and exercise (and showing off to your friends) rather than in

Heel kick

Side kick

real fights. It is dangerous to use in a fight because it leaves you unstable and almost completely open to attack.

In this kick, your body faces forward while the kick shoots out to the side. Shift your weight to the nonkicking foot, and raise the knee of the kicking foot. Strike out to the side. The ankle of the striking foot should be bent so that the outer edge of the foot hits the target. Keep your toes pointed down and back toward your body as much as possible. In some versions of the kick, you may punch or extend your arms out over the kicking leg in order to maintain balance.

ROUNDHOUSE KICK

The roundhouse kick is basically a side kick that comes from behind and swings toward the front, rather than shooting straight out to the side. The name *roundhouse* seems to be a translation of a Japanese term that has become widely popular. In traditional kungfu, this kick was known as the sweeping side kick.

Roundhouse kick

INSIDE WORK: MIND AND SPIRIT

The "inside" work of kungfu has three main parts: disciplining the mind, improving your vital energy (what the Chinese call *qi*), and developing virtue (what you might call how to become a hero).

Disciplining the Mind

In kungfu, training your mind is even more important than training your body. With concentration, you learn quickly. With self-control and self-confidence, you can put what you learn to good use. These skills will be valuable to you throughout your life.

Have you ever had trouble with your mind getting out of control? Does it sometimes behave like a wild horse, running in every direction except forward? For example, when you should be doing your homework, does your mind wander to other topics, like playing your favorite video game? Or in class, when you really want to do your best, do you get nervous and completely forget the answers? The ability to keep your mind focused on what you want to do is called concentration. Clearly, it is a very useful skill.

Similarly, does your mind sometimes behave like a volcano, exploding when something goes wrong? Perhaps you get angry or disappointed or frustrated and then do things that lead to big trouble. Clearly, it would be better if you could stay calm and ignore little problems. This ability is called self-control. Like concentration, it, too, is clearly very useful in many parts of your life.

Another situation when your mind can help you is when someone insults you or calls you names. They are trying to make you angry! You may want to fight, but if you get angry, then you are doing what they want. A better way is to have the self-confidence and quick mind to be able to answer them or act in a way that will make them leave you alone.

So, how can you develop these mental powers of concentration, self-control, and self-confidence? You train the mind exactly the way you train the body: You practice a certain quality, and as you practice it, the quality becomes stronger in your character, just like a muscle grows in your body.

In training the mind, there are basically two steps:

1. Give your mind an assignment. Decide what you want it to focus on, then put your full attention there.

2. When you find your mind has wandered, bring it back to the assignment. Do not blame yourself or some other person or thing; just return to the assignment—again and again.

You can train the mind at any time. Training the mind while the body is not moving has a special name: meditation. There are many ways to meditate. Sometimes people sit cross-legged; kungfu practitioners sometimes meditate in the horse stance. There are also many "assignments," depending on the style of meditation. For example, the assignment might be "Count your breaths from one to ten. When you reach ten, start over with one. Keep going." The assignment is always simple, and it often involves the breath.

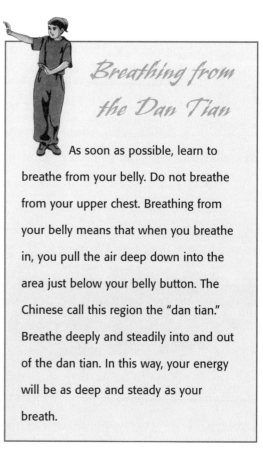

Breathing from the Dan Tian

As soon as possible, learn to breathe from your belly. Do not breathe from your upper chest. Breathing from your belly means that when you breathe in, you pull the air deep down into the area just below your belly button. The Chinese call this region the "dan tian." Breathe deeply and steadily into and out of the dan tian. In this way, your energy will be as deep and steady as your breath.

Training the mind while the body is active is the same. You have an assignment and try to stick to it. The assignment is to think *only* about what you are doing at that moment. Delivering a thrust kick? Moving into forward stance? Brushing your teeth? Whatever it is, give it your full attention. Notice every detail about what you are doing—and nothing else.

Of course, whether your body is moving or not, your mind will soon jump somewhere else. When you notice that it has wandered, just go back to the assignment. You do *not* blame yourself; you do *not* blame your neighbor; you do *not* feel like a failure; you do *not* wish you could do something else—all of these thoughts are *not* part of the assignment! Instead you just go back to your assignment. As you bring your mind back to the assignment, again and again and again, the mind becomes strong. Through this exercise, concentration, determination, self-control, patience, and even self-confidence naturally and automatically grow.

Improving Qi

The idea that living bodies have a special invisible energy is common in both Western and Eastern cultures. The Chinese call this energy *qi*. They believe that in humans it is stored just below the belly button, in a region they call the *dan tian*. From the dan tian, qi circulates in special pathways through the body. When the flow is smooth and strong, the body is healthy and the mind is clear. Exercises to promote the flow of qi are part of advanced kungfu training. As a beginner, don't think about it. We mention it because you might hear these terms mentioned and wonder what they have to do with kungfu.

How to Become a Hero: Developing Virtue

Great martial artists are also great people. They are respected and admired by their friends and neighbors for being honest, loyal, wise, and responsible. They are not feared and hated because they are likely to beat up anyone who crosses their path.

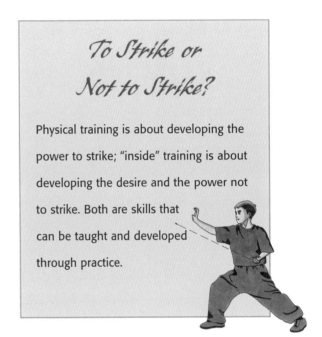

To Strike or Not to Strike?

Physical training is about developing the power to strike; "inside" training is about developing the desire and the power not to strike. Both are skills that can be taught and developed through practice.

Developing this kind of virtue is also a part of martial arts training. Virtue naturally grows when you meditate, study, and associate with fine people—like your teachers. It also comes from following the rules of the school. By practicing respect for your teachers and your fellow students, you develop humility. By obeying the rules, you develop discipline. By helping younger students, you develop compassion. Long hours of practice will give you patience and self-respect. This is how you become not only a great martial artist but also a great human being.

Six

PRACTICING KUNGFU WITH FORMS

Each style of kungfu has its own set of forms that have been passed from master to student over many years. Forms have four basic purposes.

The first purpose is to help students develop their kungfu skills. By performing the forms, students learn flexibility, coordination, balance, and timing. They learn to use one movement after another, for example, moving smoothly from a horse stance, to an uppercut, to a down block. Repeating the forms builds strength, endurance, and familiarity.

The second purpose is to help the teacher. The forms are like textbooks and tests because they represent different levels of difficulty. The teacher can use them to teach step by step and to evaluate the progress of a student.

The third purpose of forms is to preserve the specific techniques of kungfu. Many years ago, kungfu techniques were not writ-ten down; they were preserved only in the minds of people. But how to make sure the students would remember everything, and remember it precisely? Just as in a language it's easier to remember a ten-word sentence than a list of ten words, so in kungfu, the masters discovered that their students could remember movements better if they were strung together. Martial arts forms become "sentences" that masters created to help students remember their special techniques and to ensure that the techniques would be preserved for future generations.

A fourth purpose of forms is for demonstration and entertainment. In the old days in China, martial arts were performed as entertainment in front of audiences, sometimes in the street and sometimes in theaters. Even today, people everywhere appreciate and enjoy watching the skill and gracefulness of good kungfu.

Opera Saves Kungfu!

During one period in Chinese history, the emperor forbade martial arts because he was afraid the martial artists would train others to rebel against him. So martial artists became opera stars, and many operas based on kungfu themes were created and performed. Thus, the kungfu artists were able to keep up their skills by practicing onstage!

HOW TO LEARN FORMS

Here are some guidelines for learning a form.

Memorize it. First, just learn the sequence: memorize what comes first, second, third, and so on. Keep practicing until you can go from start to finish without stopping.

Make it perfect. Once you know the sequence, try to make each movement perfect. Do not rush. Do not let your movements be sloppy. Each part of the form should be clear and exact.

Smooth out the transitions. Next, concentrate on smoothness. After you can do each individual movement perfectly, pay attention to connecting them. Try to move from one movement to the next very smoothly.

Develop power and speed. Finally, focus your attention on power and speed. If you have done all the previous steps, then power and speed will come automatically. When one motion naturally connects with the next, power also naturally flows, just like water rushing down a hillside.

FIVE ANIMAL EXERCISES

The Five Animal Exercises in this chapter are typical forms; they are simplified versions of traditional Shaolin Temple exercises. In order to do the exercises, you must

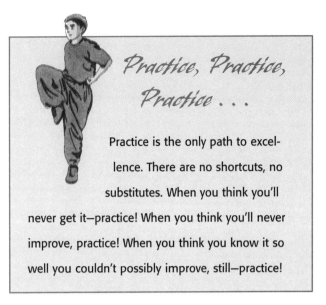

Practice, Practice, Practice . . .

Practice is the only path to excellence. There are no shortcuts, no substitutes. When you think you'll never get it—practice! When you think you'll never improve, practice! When you think you know it so well you couldn't possibly improve, still—practice!

know the basic elements described in Chapter 5. Read the directions carefully and follow the illustrations. If you have trouble, ask someone to read the directions to you while you do the movements. Step by step, you can figure out what to do. Good luck!

The five animals are: tiger, leopard, crane, snake, and dragon. The early kungfu masters thought that these animals represented the five most important qualities of a good kungfu fighter. As you do each exercise, pretend you are that animal—imagine how it fights and imitate its motions. In this way, your movements will be beautiful and very powerful, and your body will grow strong.

Tiger

For the Chinese, the tiger is the king of the beasts (just like Western people think of the lion, but China has no lions). He is ferocious! His claws rip and tear! So, when you do the tiger form, make your eyes angry, be bold and fierce; you may even growl with each strike. It is believed that doing the tiger form will make your bones as strong as iron.

Leopard

The leopard is as fierce as the tiger, but it is smaller, stronger, and faster. Speed is the big difference. When you do the leopard form, imagine yourself smooth and sleek. With your hand movements, punch rather than rip. Doing the leopard form will develop muscular strength to match the bone strength you get from the tiger form.

Crane

For the Chinese, the crane represents long life. It is a graceful bird that has a long neck, wide wings, and a powerful beak. It also has perfect balance: it can stand on one leg for hours. So, when you do the crane form, feel graceful, stay balanced, and strike very precisely. Doing the crane form will improve your balance, concentration, and endurance.

Snake

The snake is cool and calm, never showing anger or fear. But in times of danger, it strikes with lightning speed and deadly poison. When you do the snake form, make your movements very smooth (remember that the snake has no arms or legs!), and then strike suddenly with perfect accuracy. Doing the snake form will improve your self-control and internal energy, known as qi.

Dragon

The dragon is unique among the five animals because it is not real. Also, the Chinese dragon differs from the Western dragon in important ways. The Chinese dragon is not fierce and does not breathe fire. Instead, it is associated with water, both lakes and oceans and the clouds in the sky. It can appear and disappear, grow big or small, as it likes. So when you do the dragon form, imagine that you are a mythical beast: use your waist to move your body like a dragon swinging its tail, and let your movements be sudden and surprising. Doing the dragon form will develop your inner spirit.

THE EXERCISES

Note on the illustrations: The numbers of the illustrations and the text match. Arrows show how to get to the next position. So, for example, when you finish doing the instructions of Snake position 2, you will look like the illustration Snake position 2. The arrows in the Snake position 2 illustration show how to get to Snake position 3.

READY POSITION

Stand in this position to start each of the Five Animal Exercises: feet together, hands as fists at your waist, shoulders down, spine straight, tall, and alert.

SNAKE

Start in ready position. Make the snake hand with both hands. To make the snake hand, your thumb overlaps the fourth and fifth fingers while your first and second fingers point forward. Keep both hands as snake hands throughout the exercise.

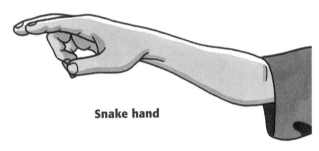

Snake hand

Snake position 1

1. Step forward on your right foot into a right forward stance. As you step, your right arm blocks upward from left to right in front of your chest. At the end, the palm of your right snake hand is facing your right shoulder; your left is still at your waist.

Ready position, front and side views

Snake position 1

Snake position 2

2. Your left hand strikes out (palm facing down). At the same time, your right hand draws back to your right shoulder (palm facing inward). Do not move your feet.

Snake position 2

Snake position 3

3. Your right hand then strikes forward (palm down). At the same time, your left hand pulls back to a position under your right elbow (palm down).

To end, relax and step either forward or back to ready position, or continue with steps 4–8 for the advanced version.

4. Your right hand blocks to the left (palm facing in), your right arm bent at the elbow. The left hand stays still, under your right forearm.

5. Your right hand strikes to the front (palm down). Your left hand stays still, under your right elbow.

6. Step forward into a left front stance (left foot forward). At the same time, your left hand circles counterclockwise in front of

Snake position 3

your chest as your right hand pulls back to the waist (palm up).

7. Your left hand strikes to the front (palm down). Your right hand doesn't move.

8. Your right hand strikes to the front (palm down) as your left hand pulls back to a position under your right elbow.

Finally, bring your right foot up to meet the left, returning to ready position.

DRAGON

Start in ready position.

Make the dragon claw with both hands. The dragon claw is an open palm with fingers slightly spread and slightly bent. It is like the tiger claw, but the fingers are not so bent—a little more open and stretched out. Keep your hands as dragon claws for the entire exercise.

Dragon position 1

33

Dragon claw

Dragon position 1

1. Move your right foot across in front of your body (to make the cross stance). At the same time, your two hands (both as dragon claws) block down toward the lower right. Your right hand should end at the same height as your right hip, while your left hand ends at the same height as your stomach. Look toward the right. (That is, your body is moving to the left while your hands and head move to the right.)

Dragon position 2

2. Next, move your left foot across and in front of your right (to make a second cross stance). At the same time, your two hands move together, in a counterclockwise circle in front of your body. End with your left hand by your waist and your right hand in front of your left shoulder.

Dragon position 2

Dragon position 3

3. Step with your right foot in the same direction as the last cross stance to make a horse stance. Don't move your hands.

Dragon position 3

Dragon position 4

4. Next, pivot on your toes to the right, into a front stance. At the same time, shoot out your two hands—double dragon claws—directly in front of your chest. End with your right hand on top at head height and your left hand directly below, in front of

6. Move your right foot across in front of your body to make a second cross stance, as both hands circle clockwise in front of your body and then come back to right side of your waist (left hand above, right hand below).

7. Your left foot steps forward into a left forward stance as double dragon claws shoot out.

Finally, the right foot steps up to the left, returning to ready position.

LEOPARD

Start in ready position.

Make leopard fists: bend your fingers at the middle knuckle; keep your fingers tightly together so that all the knuckles line up. Put your thumb over the tip of your index finger, well tucked back from the front. Keep your hands as leopard fists throughout the exercise.

Dragon position 4

your chest. The heels of your hands should be about a hand's width apart.

To end, bring your left foot up to the right and relax into ready position, or continue for the advanced version (the advanced version has the same movements on the other side).

5. Move your left foot across in front of body to make a cross stance, as both hands block down to the left.

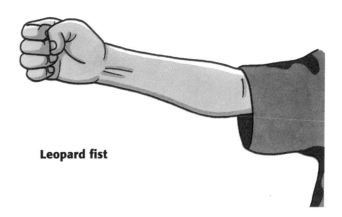

Leopard fist

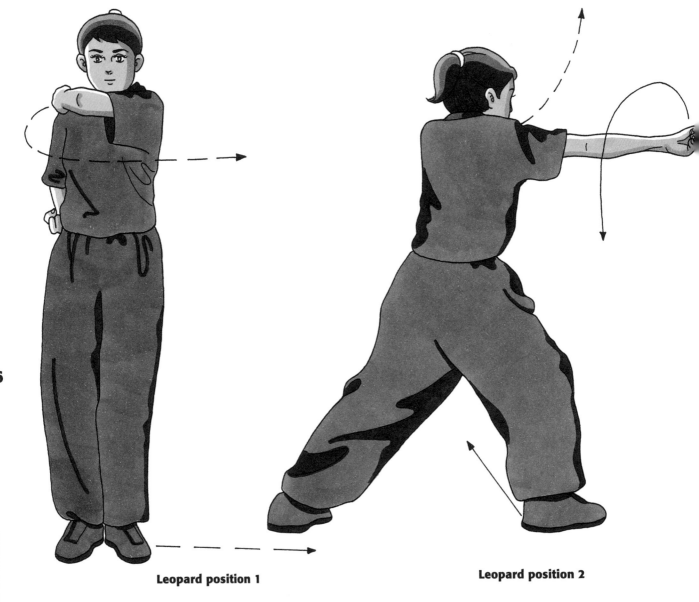

Leopard position 1

Leopard position 2

Leopard position 1

1. Raise your left hand to your right shoulder so that your elbow is horizontal in front of your chest, palm facing your body. Your left foot steps to the side into a horse stance. Look to the left and strike out with your left hand, snapping it from the elbow, striking to the left at shoulder height.

Leopard position 2

2. Your right foot steps to the left into a forward stance (in a straight line with the horse stance). At the same time, your right hand strikes to the front. As you strike, turn your hand so that the palm ends up facing out and your thumb faces down. Your left hand pulls back to your collarbone with your palm facing out.

4. From the crane stance, hop forward onto your right foot, then swing your left foot behind your right foot into a cross stance (moving forward in straight line). At the same time, your right hand shoots out to the right at shoulder height, while your left fist comes in (arm bent at the elbow), ending at the right armpit.

5. Your body turns, bringing your right hip forward as your left arm swings up and down, ending in a horse stance. Your right arm balances left, staying behind and ending stretched out at your side, just like the left arm.

6. Your right foot steps forward into another horse stance. At the same time, your right arm swings up and around from back to front, all the way down to end in front of your body (your palm facing somewhat to right). Your left arm rises at the upper left for balance with your palm out.

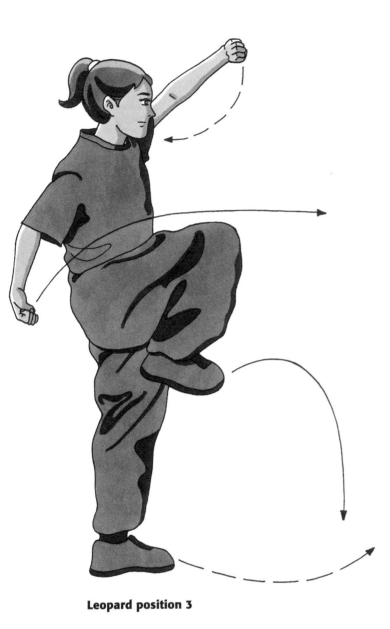

Leopard position 3

Leopard position 3

3. Your right hand blocks (swings) down to the lower right (palm facing front) while your left hand blocks to the upper left (palm facing out). At the same time, shift your weight back onto your left foot and raise your right foot into a crane stance.

To end, step forward into ready position or continue for the advanced version.

7. Shift your weight to the right into a forward stance. At the same time, your right arm strikes upward (palm up), ending at head height, while your left arm falls forward, ending under your right elbow, protecting your chest (with palm down). Finally, bring your back (left) foot forward into ready position.

TIGER

Start in ready position.

Tiger claw

Make tiger claws with both hands. The tiger claw is exactly like the eagle claw (described in Chapter 5) except that the fingers are spread apart. Keep your hands as tiger claws for the entire exercise.

Tiger position 1

1. Step forward on your right foot into a right front stance. At the same time, your right hand blocks upward, moving in a clockwise circle from the lower left to upper right in front of your chest.

Tiger position 2

2. Pull your right hand back to your waist; at the same time, your left-hand tiger claw strikes out to the center front. Don't move your feet!

Tiger position 3

3. Pivot on the heel of your right foot so that your toes point out to the side at about 45 degrees. Once your right foot is set, slide your left foot forward into a cat stance, facing front. When you make the cat stance, at the same time, pull your left hand back and strike with your right hand. The right hand strike should be at chest height, like the first movement.

To end, step down into ready position or continue for the advanced version.

Tiger position 1

Tiger position 2

Tiger position 3

4. Change direction to 90 degrees to the right by stepping sidewise into a cross stance (your left leg crosses in front of your right). As your feet move, your right hand blocks in a counterclockwise half circle downward. Don't move your left hand—it stays at your waist.

5. Step into a right front stance with your right foot. At the same time, your right arm moves in a counterclockwise circle (an inward block) in front of your chest, ending with your hand in front of your upper chest.

6. Then your left tiger claw strikes to the front as your right forearm falls back so that it is guarding your midchest. (Note: Your elbow is still outward.)

7. Pull your right tiger claw back to your waist while your left tiger claw pulls back to your right shoulder. Don't move your feet!

8. Now, turn to the left, stepping into a left front stance. (You should turn 180 degrees so that you end up facing in the opposite direction.) At the same time, both hands move: your left hand blocks down to the left, while your right hand strikes to the front at mid-chest height. Both hands end in midair in front of your body, the right above the left.

9. With your right foot, step 90 degrees to the right, into a right front stance.

At same time, your right arm blocks out to the front and your left hand pulls back to the waist. The fingers of left hand should point toward the ground.

10. Pull your right hand back to your waist. At the same time, your left-hand tiger claw strikes out to the center front. Don't move your feet!

Notice that movement 9 is the same as step 1, and step 10 is the same as step 2. So, at this point, you can either end the form by returning to ready position, or you can repeat the exercise by going back to step 3 and continuing from there.

CRANE

Start in ready position.

To make the crane's beak, bring all your fingertips (four fingers and thumb) together at one point. The fingers should curve naturally, creating a space inside. Then bend the wrist so the thumb is at a 90 degree angle with the arm.

Crane's Beak

Keep your hands as crane's beaks through the exercise (except for step 7 as indicated).

Crane position 1

Crane position 1

1. Your right foot steps diagonally forward, 45 degrees to the right, into a cat stance. At the same time, your right hand blocks upward, in a clockwise circle. As your hand Yrises, make your fingers into a crane's beak, ending at shoulder height. Your weight should be on the left foot; your left hand doesn't move. Raise your left hand to head height. As it rises, make the fingers into a crane's beak. Your hand ends up near your left ear, ready to strike. (Note: Keep both of your hands as crane's beaks for the rest of the exercise.)

Crane position 2

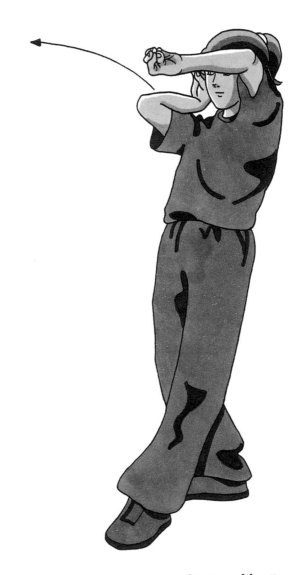

Crane position 3

Crane position 2

2. Now strike out with your left hand. Strike directly forward, at the same height as your head. As you strike, pull your right hand back to stop in front of your collarbone (upper chest). You should still be in a cat stance with your weight on your left foot.

Crane position 3

3. Shift your weight to your right foot and move left foot diagonally forward, 45 degrees, into a second cat stance (now on the other foot). At the same time, do a backward block. To do this, move your left hand in a clockwise circle with the elbow as the center. (This is the same circle that the right hand made in step 1.) At the end, the left arm is extended (with elbow bent), hand at chest height, fingers pointing to the left. Your right hand should be a crane's beak held near your right ear—ready to strike.

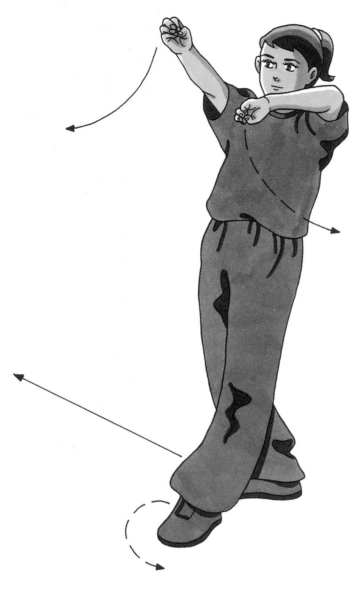

Crane position 4

6. Here, the crane spreads its wings and kicks. Open your hands wide and spread your arms to the side as your right foot kicks to the front.

7. Immediately pull the foot back to a crane stance, and make crane's beaks again with your hands.

8. Hold the crane stance while your left hand makes a big clockwise circle in front of your chest, ending with your forearm in the middle parallel to the ground. (This movement is called a middle-chest block.) At the same time, raise your right hand to head height; cock it, ready for the next strike.

9. Step forward on your right foot into a front stance.

10. Pull your left hand back to your waist, and strike down with your right hand.

11. Move your left foot up to the right as both hands return as fists to the waist.

You can either end here or immediately go back to step 1 and repeat the sequence.

Crane position 4

4. Now, pull your left hand back to your right shoulder as your right hand strikes. Don't move your feet!

To end, step forward into ready position or continue for the advanced version.

5. Step forward on your left foot into a cross stance (keep your hands still).

seven

ADVANCING IN KUNGFU

If you train regularly, you will make progress. Then what? In schools with a ranking system, you may test for promotion. In almost all schools you may enter tournaments. You may be asked to join demonstrations, especially lion dances. In addition, you may face serious discouragement and frustration. In all these cases, you can prepare to win and have fun while you do it.

TESTING FOR PROMOTION

There is no traditional ranking system in kungfu. In the past such a system was not needed. In modern schools, however, many teachers feel that a ranking system helps students by giving them specific goals and a way to measure how much they've learned.

If your school has a ranking system, find out how it works. Usually, there is a fixed set of requirements for each level. At beginning levels, the test will probably cover the basic movements (punches, kicks,

and so on). At intermediate levels, the test will probably involve doing a particular form. At advanced levels, there may be two-man sparring. Promotion tests may be regular (for example, every two months) or irregular (whenever there are enough students to test). Students perform in front of judges. Sometimes they perform individually, sometimes in a group. Usually parents and friends are welcome to watch. Testing and promotion days are often important occasions at a school—and happy ones!

"Keeper" Keys to Performing Well

Keep focused.

Keep breathing.

Keep going!

How do you prepare for a promotion test? First, know what you will be tested on. Practice it again and again. On the day of the test, arrive on time and in a clean uniform. Follow your usual warm-up routine. (Use the bathroom if you need to.) As you wait your turn, breathe slowly and deeply into your lower belly. Then, when it's your turn—keep breathing, keep calm—and do your best!

TOURNAMENTS AND COMPETITIONS

While a ranking system is not traditional in kungfu, friendly competitions are. Performing in front of an audience helps improve skills and concentration.

Today, kungfu tournaments are like sports meets. They are usually held in gymnasiums. In the center, two or three rings are marked off where the contestants perform. Judges sit at the corners or in the middle. As each event is called, the performer comes to the center, bows to the judges, says his name, and then performs. At the end, prizes are awarded. The events are divided according to age groups and according to the type of form (empty-hand forms, weapons forms, sparring).

Who goes to tournaments? Usually, your teacher chooses which tournaments the school will join and which students enter which events. When you are ready, he will ask you. If you are nervous about competing, go to a tournament first as a spectator. Then decide if you'd like to join or not.

Preparing for a tournament is basically the same as preparing for a test at your school. There are two important differences. One is size: the gymnasium and the audience will both be much bigger. The second is familiarity: you will not be familiar with the location, particularly the floor.

Here's what you can do to make sure that you will do your very best in any tournament.

1. **Practice what you will perform many times.** Do it until it becomes automatic. Do it for your family and friends, so that you get used to people watching.

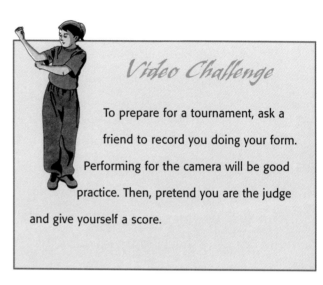

Video Challenge

To prepare for a tournament, ask a friend to record you doing your form. Performing for the camera will be good practice. Then, pretend you are the judge and give yourself a score.

2. **Try to get a very good idea of what the tournament will be like.** Ask people who have been to tournaments: How did they prepare? What surprised them? What advice can they give you? Especially, ask them about the floor. For example, sometimes a thin rug is put down over the gymnasium floor. If you usually practice on a hard surface, then you may want to try to practice on a rug just to become familiar with it.

3. **On the day of the tournament, arrive early.** Allow plenty of time to register and look around. Be prepared for lots of activity. There will be people rushing frantically here and there, children screaming, loudspeakers blaring. Find the places you will need. That means finding the ring where you will perform, the waiting area for performers, the water fountains, and the rest

rooms. Also, know where your parents and your school will be in case you need to find them.

4. Be calm. Follow your regular routine of warming up. Save your energy. Don't run around or talk too much. If your find yourself getting nervous, take a deep breath. Bring the air deep into your lower belly; then let it out slowly and evenly. Continue to breathe like this—slow, deep, and even—until you feel calm.

5. When you perform, forget the audience; forget any mistakes you might make. Think only of your teacher's form and of yourself doing the form perfectly. Enjoy!

DEMONSTRATIONS AND LION DANCES

Many kungfu schools are asked to give performances at community festivals. Schools of southern kungfu styles may be asked to perform the lion dance. The "lion" is a huge head, made of bamboo and papier-mâché, with a long, wide piece of cloth behind it representing the lion's body. All of it is brightly decorated. One person carries the head while a second person is under the tail. The two work together to make the lion look real—running, jumping, and playing. The lion dances to the beat of a drum, cymbals, and a gong, and these instruments are also played by members of the kungfu school.

Performing the lion dance is a great honor—and hard work. The performers must practice long hours to develop strong muscles as well as endurance, timing, and coordination.

WHEN YOU FEEL LIKE QUITTING

If you train regularly, you will certainly make progress. But at some point you will almost certainly feel discouraged. For example, you may suddenly feel like there's too much to learn, you can't get it, and other students always do better than you, anyway. Or maybe there's not enough to learn, or it's all too boring. Basically, you just feel like quitting.

This is a real problem!

Before you really do quit, think carefully. Think about where you were the day you joined, and where you are now. What progress, right? You have to stop to see it. Are other people doing better than you? That will always be true. There will always be someone better than you—and someone worse than you. The difference between you and them doesn't matter. What matters is the difference between you before and you now: your improvement. Boring? Get reinspired by looking at what people ahead of you are doing and by talking to them. Keep working and you'll get there too!

eight

WHAT KUNGFU CAN DO FOR YOU

Kungfu is lifelong training. It can help you at every stage of your life. Here are some of the benefits waiting for you.

BODY

As you train you should find yourself becoming faster, stronger, more flexible, more coordinated, and better able to keep your balance.

Are you doing the Five Animal Exercises? If so, then according to the old masters, you will develop hard bones like a tiger, strong muscles like a leopard, unwavering balance like a crane, cool concentration like a snake, and the vibrant spirit of a dragon!

MIND

As you train, you should find yourself becoming better able to concentrate, better able to stick to a task until it's finished, more even-tempered (less likely to get angry or upset), and more confident in your own abilities.

Whether you need to be fierce like a tiger, cool like a snake, unpredictable like a dragon, or as steadfast as a crane, you will have the quality needed.

SPIRIT

As you train, you should find yourself becoming simply a better person—more honest, trustworthy, loyal, responsible, and even fun to be with—everyone will like to call you friend!

Like the five animals, you will become more true to yourself.

In a nutshell, kungfu should make you feel *great!*

NOTE TO PARENTS

You are a critical part of your child's kungfu training. Your attitude will greatly influence how much and what kind of benefit your child experiences as he or she trains. While your child probably wants to learn kungfu for the fun of it (and it *is* fun!), there are other dimensions that are even more important for the long run. Basic human virtues (e.g., integrity, respect, self-discipline) and valuable mental skills (concentration, patience, and perseverance to name a few) are as much a part of the kungfu tradition as kicking and punching.

But it is up to teachers and parents to ensure young students get the full benefit. Parents can help in three ways.

First, choose a school that embodies the characteristics you want your child to develop. While you evaluate practical characteristics (and your child is evaluating the cool moves going on) also consider what kind of people you find at the school—both teachers and, especially, longtime students. Are these people you want your kids to emulate? Consider character along with credentials, cost, and convenience.

Second, provide informed support. "Children are not miniature adults," as one wise martial arts educator has observed. They are physically and emotionally different. Hence, they actually need to train a little differently; they respond to new experiences differently; and they will change as their minds and bodies develop—sometimes irregularly. Knowing this, you can help them weather the rough spots and stick with the training. (For a more complete description and very practical advice, the book *The Young Martial Arts Enthusiast* by David Mitchell is highly recommended.)

Third, provide moral guidance. If you want your child to grow into the moral dimension of kungfu, then use opportunities that arise to instill these attitudes. For example, help him or her understand that kungfu is really about learning to *avoid* conflict, not looking for opportunities to fight; that tournaments are about competing, not winning; that routine and rituals (like the salute) are part of learning discipline, etc. In this way, your young martial artist will gain lifelong benefit from the training.

OTHER TITLES IN THE
TUTTLE MARTIAL ARTS FOR KIDS SERIES

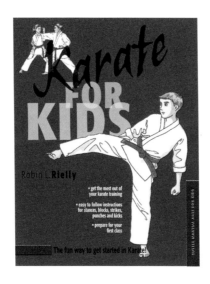

ISBN: 0 8048 3534 9

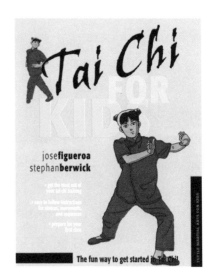

ISBN: 0 8048 3563 2

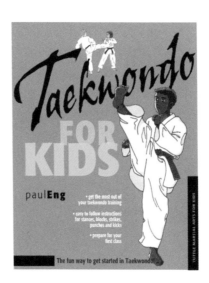

ISBN: 0 8048 3631 0